# COOL PRINTMAKING

BILLINGS COUNTY PUBLIC SCHOOL
Box 307
Medora, North Dakota 58645

## THE ART OF CREATIVITY FOR KIDS!

ANDERS HANSON

ABDO
Publishing Company

# CONTENTS

Published by ABDO Publishing Company, 8000 West 78th Street, Edina, Minnesota 55439.

Copyright © 2009 by Abdo Consulting Group, Inc. International copyrights reserved in all countries.

No part of this book may be reproduced in any form without written permission from the publisher. Checkerboard Library™ is a trademark and logo of ABDO Publishing Company.

Printed in the United States.

Editor: Pam Price

Series Concept: Nancy Tuminelly

Cover and Interior Design: Anders Hanson, Mighty Media

Photo Credits: Anders Hanson, Shutterstock

Library of Congress Cataloging-in-Publication Data

Hanson, Anders, 1980-

   Cool printmaking : the art of creativity for kids / Anders Hanson.

      p. cm. -- (Cool art)

   Includes index.

   ISBN 978-1-60453-147-3

1. Prints--Technique--Juvenile literature. I. Title.

NE860.H36 2008

760.28--dc22

2008022323

## Get the Picture!

When a step number in an activity has a colored circle around it, look for the picture that goes with it. The picture's border will be the same color as the circle.

2 ·········>

# THE ART OF creativity

## You Are Creative

Being creative is all about using your imagination to make new things. Coming up with new ideas and bringing them to life is part of being human. Everybody is creative! Creative thinking takes time and practice. But that's okay, because being creative is a lot of fun!

## Calling All Artists

Maybe you believe that you aren't good at art. Maybe you have some skills that you want to improve. The purpose of this book is to help you develop your visual creativity. Remember that your artistic skills improve every time you make art. The activities in this book can help you become the creative artist you want to be!

### Creativity Tips

- Stay positive.
- There is no wrong way to be creative.
- Allow yourself to make mistakes.
- Tracing isn't cheating.
- Practice, practice, practice.
- Be patient.
- Have fun!

# Printmaking is cool!

*Creativity takes courage.*
—Henri Matisse

## What Is Printmaking?

Printmaking is the art of creating prints. To make a print, an artist first creates an image on a surface called a printing plate. The print is made when the artist transfers the image from the plate onto a piece of paper. The cool thing about printmaking is that you can often make many prints from each plate.

A printing plate can be made of various materials. Wood, stone, metal, and fabric are just a few examples. The methods used to create an image on the plate are different for each type of printmaking. The four major types of printmaking are relief, intaglio, stencil, and planographic. See pages 12 and 13 to learn about the **techniques** used in each style of printmaking.

PRINTING PLATE

PRINT

## Early Printmaking

Prehistoric humans were printmakers. Early artists placed their hands against cave walls and blew colored dust around them. When they removed their hands, the outlines remained on the cave walls.

## Be a Printmaker!

Printmaking is fun because you can make lots of copies of your art. Friends and family members love to get original art. With printmaking, you can make enough copies for all of them!

If you are not satisfied with your first prints, remember this. Great artists are not always satisfied with their work. Part of what makes them great is that they are always trying to get better. You don't need to be good at art now to become a great artist. You just need the desire to learn and become better!

***BLOCK-CUTTER AT WORK** (1568)*
*—JOST AMMAN*

## Don't Be a Judge!

When discussing a work of art, avoid using the words listed below. They offer judgments without saying much about the character of the work. Instead, look at how the artist used composition and techniques. Try to understand what the artist was trying to achieve. See pages 8 through 13 to read about these elements.

- good
- bad
- right
- wrong
- silly
- stupid

## Have Patience

Be patient with yourself. Changes won't happen overnight. When you make a print that you don't like, don't throw it out. Save it so you can look back later and see how much you've improved! Have **confidence** in yourself. You can do anything you set your mind to!

# TOOLS OF THE TRADE

WATER-BASED PRINTING INKS

SOFT RUBBER BRAYER

FRESH LEAVES

PAPER TOWELS

WHOLE FISH

FOAM PLATE

SPONGE BRUSH

PAINTBRUSH

SPOON

NEWSPAPER

Each activity in this book has a list of the tools and materials you will need. When you come across a tool you don't know, turn back to these pages. You can find most of these items at your local art store.

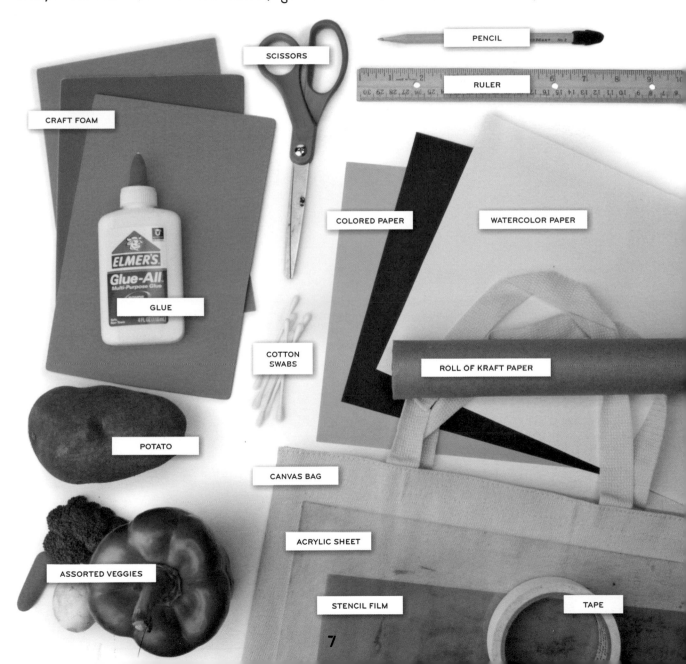

SCISSORS

PENCIL

RULER

CRAFT FOAM

COLORED PAPER

WATERCOLOR PAPER

GLUE

COTTON SWABS

ROLL OF KRAFT PAPER

POTATO

CANVAS BAG

ASSORTED VEGGIES

ACRYLIC SHEET

STENCIL FILM

TAPE

# Basic Elements

These are the elements that make up images. All prints can be described by these key **concepts**.

## Point

The point is the most basic element of visual art. The method used to create a point is different for each style of printmaking.

## Line

Connecting two points creates a line. Lines can be straight, angled, or curved. They may be thick or thin. Lines can be hard and rigid or soft and sketchy.

## Shape

When lines enclose a space, they create a shape. A shape can be **geometric**, such as a circle or a square, or **irregular**. Shapes may be empty or solid.

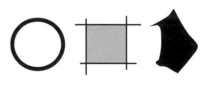

## Pattern

Points, lines, and shapes can create a pattern when they repeat in an organized and **predictable** way.

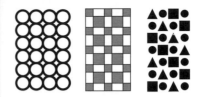

## Texture

You can create texture by repeating points, lines, or shapes. Make them so small that you can't easily see the individual elements.

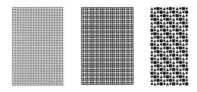

## Value

Value describes how light or dark a color is. Light objects have little value. Dark objects have a lot of value.

LIGHT ← → DARK

## Color

You can make every color by mixing the primary colors. Mixing any two primary colors creates a secondary color.

COLOR WHEEL

PRIMARY COLORS
Red    Yellow    Blue

SECONDARY COLORS
Orange    Green    Violet

# Composition

Bringing together the basic elements to make a work of art is called composition.
The following ideas will help you create great compositions!

## Focal Point

The focal point is the first thing you see when you look at a print. Without a focal point, a print may seem **chaotic**.

FOCUSED

UNFOCUSED

## Balance

Balance refers to the arrangement of elements in a print. Evenly spread objects create balance. Objects grouped in one area create an unbalanced composition.

BALANCED

UNBALANCED

## Movement

Movement occurs when things appear to be traveling across a print. The image on the left moves like a river. The one on the right feels calm, like a lake.

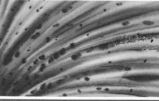

MOVEMENT

STILLNESS

## Space

Whenever lines enclose a space, two shapes are made. The shape inside the lines is called positive space. The shape outside the lines is called negative space. When these shapes work well together, the composition is more interesting.

POSITIVE SPACE

NEGATIVE SPACE

NEGATIVE SPACE

## Rhythm

Rhythm isn't just for musicians! Artists repeat elements to give their work rhythm.

RHYTHMIC LINES

## Harmony

When two or more elements in a print share **characteristics**, they are in **harmony**. When elements don't have much in common, they are **dissonant**. Characteristics that help create harmony include color, size, and shape.

HARMONIC SHAPES

DISSONANT SHAPES

## Contrast

Contrast occurs when art has both extremes of an element. Using smooth and rough textures, light and dark values, and large and small shapes are ways to add contrast.

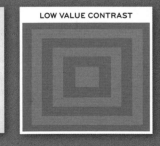

LOW VALUE CONTRAST

HIGH VALUE CONTRAST

# Techniques

There are four major types of printmaking. Each one uses a different **technique**.

## Relief Printing

Relief printing is the process of making prints from a raised surface. First the artist cuts away the unwanted part of the surface. Only the design remains. Then the artist puts ink on the raised surface. The ink is then transferred to paper or another material. Common surfaces used for relief printing plates are wood, linoleum, and metal.

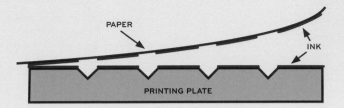

### Types of relief printing

- woodcut
- linocut
- stamping
- fish printing

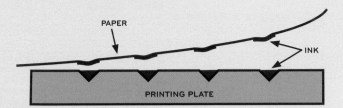

### Types of intaglio printing

- etching
- engraving
- drypoint
- aquatint
- mezzotint

## Intaglio Printing

Intaglio (in-TAL-yo) printing involves engraving, or cutting, a design into a printing plate. The artist forces ink into the cuts and wipes off the extra. Next, he or she applies a damp piece of paper to the plate. Finally, the artist applies pressure so the ink filling the lines of the design is pressed onto the paper.

# Stenciling

In stenciling, ink is forced through the printing plate. One form of stenciling is screen printing, also called silk screen or serigraphy. The ink will pass through areas of the screen that are not blocked by a stencil, glue, or varnish. The artist pushes the ink through with a squeegee. There is a separate screen for each ink color.

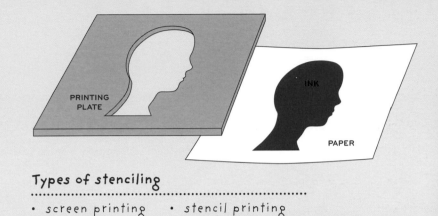

## Types of stenciling
..............................................................
- screen printing
- stencil printing

# Planographic Printing

In planographic printing, a print is made from a specially treated flat surface. The treated areas of the printing plate will hold ink. The remaining areas will refuse ink.

Lithography is a method of planographic printing that most commercial printers use. In lithography, the printer applies an oily material to the areas to be printed. The rest is treated with a material that attracts water. First the printer applies water, then ink. The ink will stick only to the oily area.

## Types of planographic printing
..............................................................
- lithography
- monoprinting

# MONOPRINT

*Just one can be fun!*

## Stuff You'll Need

Water-based printing inks, sheet of acrylic plastic, paintbrush, cotton swabs, watercolor paper, paper towels, spoon or brayer

## Print Type

Planographic

1 Choose the colors of ink you want to use. Squirt some of each onto the acrylic sheet.

2 Push the inks around the acrylic sheet with the paintbrush. Cover the entire surface with a thin layer of ink.

3 Remove some ink with cotton swabs. You can draw shapes or images with the swabs. Or, you can make marks that express how you're feeling.

4 Place the watercolor paper under slowly running water for about thirty seconds. Soak both sides. Blot the paper with a paper towel. Set the paper on top of the acrylic sheet.

## Setting Up

- Cover your workspace with newspaper, paper towels, or cardboard. This will protect your workspace from drips and splatters.

- Give yourself enough space to work.

- Place your printmaking tools within arm's reach.

- Work in a well-lit area.

- Use a plastic cup filled with water for rinsing brushes. You can dry wet brushes with extra paper towels.

5 Rub the paper with the back of a spoon or a clean, dry brayer. Try to keep the paper from moving around as you rub it.

6 You can check the progress of the print by carefully lifting an edge of the paper. If the print hasn't transferred well, replace the paper and continue rubbing.

7 Carefully peel the paper off the acrylic sheet. Allow it to dry in a safe place.

# LEAFY GIFT WRAP

**Make an impression with this artful wrapping paper!**

### Stuff You'll Need
Assortment of fresh leaves, roll
of kraft paper, scrap paper, water-based
printing ink or acrylic paint, paintbrush, foam plate

**Print Type**
Relief

1  Pick some fresh leaves. Look for leaves that are whole and have visible veins. Fresh leaves are more flexible, and the veins show up better. Find leaves that are different sizes and shapes.

2  Put several colors of ink on a foam plate.

3  Use the paintbrush to apply an even coat of ink on the back of a leaf.

4  Place the leaf ink side down on the kraft paper. Lay a clean piece of scrap paper over the leaf.

5  Use your fingers to smooth the paper over the leaf so you get a good impression.

6  Remove the scrap paper. Slowly and carefully lift up the leaf.

7  Repeat steps 3 through 6 until the paper is mostly covered. Try using different leaves and ink colors.

# POTATO PEOPLE

Create wacky characters with various veggies!

## Stuff You'll Need

Potato, assorted veggies, paper towels, water-based printing ink or acrylic paint, foam plate, spoon, paintbrush, paper

## Print Type

Relief

1   Ask an adult to cut a large potato in half lengthwise. You'll also need thick slices of other vegetables, such as green pepper and mushroom. Dry the veggies with a paper towel.

2   Choose several colors of ink. Pour a little of these colors onto a foam plate.

3   You will use the flat side of one potato half to print the face. Use a spoon to scoop out two holes for the eyes. Brush the flat side of the potato with the color you want for the face.

4   Firmly press the potato onto the paper. Lift the potato carefully off the paper to reveal the print. You may want to practice a few times on scrap paper to figure out how much ink and pressure you'll need to apply.

5   Use the other vegetables to make the rest of the person. Be creative. Think about how the different vegetables could be used to make features of the face or the body. Refer to the photos below to see what kinds of printed shapes some veggies can make.

| BROCCOLI | MINI CARROT | SLICED GREEN PEPPER | SLICED MUSHROOM CAP |

# FISH PRINT

Create colorful impressions of fresh fish!

## Gyotaku

In the 1860s, Japanese fishermen began making impressions of the prize fish they caught. The fisherman would cover the fish with ink and then lay rice paper over it to make the impression. This practice is called *gyotaku*, which means "fish impression" in Japanese. Gyotaku is still practiced today.

## Stuff You'll Need

Whole fish, paper towel, newspaper, water-based printing inks, paintbrush, foam plate, paper

## Print Type

Relief

1. If the fish is frozen, allow it to thaw. Blot the fish with a paper towel. Place the fish on newspaper.

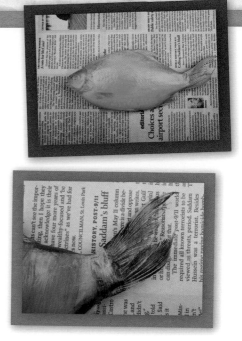

2. Choose the colored inks you want to use. Put some of each on a foam plate. The ink should be thick and tacky. If it's too watery, the print won't have much detail.

3. Coat one side of the fish with any color of ink, except black. Apply a thin, even layer of ink.

4. Load your brush with black ink. Dab the brush on a paper towel to remove excess ink. Using quick, light strokes, brush any raised areas with black ink. Your strokes should be light enough that many of the sunken areas are left unchanged.

5. Your printing paper should be thin and flexible. Rice paper works best. To make a print, place the paper on top of the inked side of the fish. Gently rub the paper into the fish with your fingers. Try to keep the paper from shifting.

6. Before removing the paper completely, lift one side to check the print. You may notice some areas that have not printed well. If so, replace the paper and rub those areas with your fingers.

7. When you're ready, remove the paper. It will be wrinkled from being pressed into the fish. That's okay, it's part of fish printing.

8. Paint a small white dot inside the eye. This helps the fish print seem more lifelike.

# WHAT A RELIEF!

Make plenty of prints from just one plate!

## Stuff You'll Need

Foam plate or tray, scissors, dull pencil or ballpoint pen, water-based printing inks, acrylic sheet or old cookie sheet, soft rubber brayer, paper, spoon

## Print Type

Relief

1. The foam tray or plate will be your printing plate. Cut off the edges so you have a flat surface to print with.

2. Draw your image on the printing plate with a dull pencil or a ballpoint pen. You'll need to draw each line with enough pressure to create an impression in the foam. If you use too much pressure, the foam will tear. If you don't use enough pressure, the plate won't print clearly.

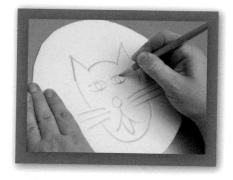

3. Put some ink onto an acrylic sheet or an old cookie sheet. Use the brayer to spread the ink into a thin, even layer. You want an even coat of ink on the brayer.

4. Roll the brayer over the printing plate in all directions until it is covered evenly with ink. If the ink is too thick, it will fill in the engraved lines. If the ink is too thin, you will get an uneven, light print.

5. Gently lay a sheet of paper on top of the inked plate. Use the back of a spoon or a clean brayer to press the paper onto the plate. This will help transfer the ink to the paper. You can lift up just a corner of the paper to check the print. When you are happy with the print, slowly peel the paper off the plate.

6. Repeat the process until you have several prints. If you want to print in a different color, wash and dry the plate and the brayer between prints.

# SUN AND MOON

Create day and night with just a few stamps!

## Stuff You'll Need

Craft foam, scissors, glue, cardboard, water-based printing inks, foam plate, light blue paper, paintbrush, pencil, dark blue or black paper

## Print Type

Relief

# The Sun Print

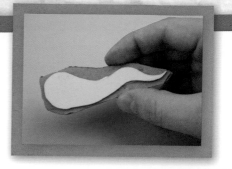

1. Cut a wavy shape out of craft foam. One end should be wide and rounded. The other end should be skinny and pointy. Glue the shape to a piece of cardboard. The cardboard should be slightly larger than the foam shape. Now you have a stamp that looks like a wavy ray of light!

2. Cut a cloud shape out of craft foam. Glue it to a slightly larger piece of cardboard.

3. Put some white, red, yellow, and orange inks on the foam plate. Get out a sheet of light blue paper.

4. Brush the cloud stamp with a thin, even layer of white ink. Try to avoid getting ink on the cardboard.

5. Press the stamp onto the paper with your fingers. Try to keep it from moving as you press down. Lift the stamp straight up. Repeat steps four and five until you have as many clouds as you like.

6. Choose a color for your wavy stamp. Brush the foam with a thin, even layer of ink.

7. Place the stamp so the wide end is near the middle of your paper. The skinny end should point away from the middle. Press the stamp onto the paper with your fingers.

8. Repeat steps six and seven until you've formed a circular pattern at the center of the paper. Allow the stamped shapes to overlap. Vary your color choices.

BILLINGS COUNTY PUBLIC SCHOOL
Box 307
Medora, North Dakota 59645

# The Moon Print

1. Cut a large circle out of craft foam. Punch out many holes of different sizes with a sharp pencil. The holes will look like craters on the moon. Glue the circle to a piece of cardboard. The cardboard should be slightly larger than the foam shape.

2. Cut three star shapes out of foam. Make them different sizes. They should all be smaller than the moon. Glue each star to a piece of cardboard. The cardboard should be slightly larger than the star you're gluing to it.

3. Put some white and some yellow ink on the foam plate. Get out a sheet of dark blue or black paper.

4. Brush the moon stamp with a thin, even layer of white ink. Try to avoid getting ink on the cardboard.

5. Set the moon stamp in the center of the paper. Press the stamp onto the paper with your fingers. Try to keep it from moving as you press down. Lift the stamp straight up.

6. Mix the remaining white ink with the yellow ink. Brush the star stamps with a thin, even layer of the mixed ink. Try to avoid getting ink on the cardboard. Stamp each star shape around the moon.

7. Continue to ink and stamp the star shapes until you've covered most of your paper.

# STENCIL STYLE

Show off your printmaking skills with this cool, creative bag!

## Stuff You'll Need

Stencil film or plastic sheet protector, ruler, scissors, pencil, water-based printing ink or acrylic paint, foam plate, tape, plain canvas bag, sponge brush

## Print Type

Stenciling

1   This project requires three stencils. One stencil is for the colorful squares, one is for the penguin's body, and one is for the penguin's white stomach. To make the stencils, first cut two 3-inch (7.6 cm) squares and one 4-inch (10.2 cm) square out of stencil film.

2   Trace the outline of one of the small squares onto the large square.

3   Trace the outline of the penguin shown here onto one of the small squares. Don't trace the oval on its belly.

4   Trace the oval of the penguin's stomach onto the other small square.

5   Now it's time to cut out the inner part of each stencil. Cut through the side of each stencil to access the inside of the stencil. Cut out the traced shape with the scissors.

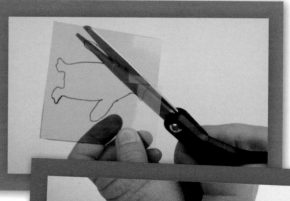

6   Tape each stencil back together.

7   Squirt several colors of ink onto the foam plate.

8   Tape the large square stencil to the center of the bag.

**9** Load the sponge brush with a colored ink of your choice. Hold the stencil in place. Dab the ink into the stencil with short, bouncy strokes. Start with the edges and move toward the center.

**10** Once you've completely filled in the square, remove the stencil. Clean the brush and the stencil with warm water. Then tape the stencil next to the square you just printed.

**11** Repeat steps 9 and 10 until you've covered most of the bag with colored squares.

**12** Squirt some black ink onto the foam plate. Line up the penguin stencil over one of the colored squares. Dab black ink into the stencil until the inside is completely covered. Repeat this process for each square. Allow the ink to dry.

**13** Squirt some white ink onto the foam plate. Line up the oval stencil over the belly of one of the penguins. Dab white ink into the stencil until the inside is completely covered. Repeat this process for each penguin.

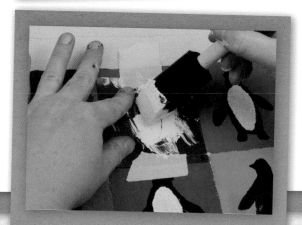

# What's next?

## Taking Care of Your Prints

Caring for prints is easy. Use the tips below to help protect your art.

- If you have a lot of loose prints, consider buying an inexpensive cardboard portfolio to keep them in. You can find one at any art store. And, they actually work better than the expensive leather portfolios!

- Put extra sheets of paper between the prints in your portfolio. This will prevent them from rubbing against each other.

## Try Something New!

The activities in this book are just a few examples of fun printmaking projects you can do. Once you've completed them all, try some of the projects again with different materials or subjects. Then make up some projects of your own!

## Advanced Printmaking

Some types of printmaking require expensive equipment. Others use dangerous chemicals or sharp tools. If you're ready for a serious challenge, you might want to explore some of these **techniques** with an adult.

- aquatint
- drypoint
- etching
- linocut
- lithography
- screen printing
- woodcut

# GLOSSARY

**chaotic** – of or relating to a state of total confusion.

**characteristic** – a quality or a feature of something.

**concept** – an idea.

**confidence** – a feeling of faith in your own abilities.

**dissonant** – having parts that don't go well together.

**geometric** – made up of straight lines, circles, and other simple shapes.

**harmony** – having parts that go well together.

**irregular** – lacking symmetry or evenness.

**predictable** – being able to guess the outcome of an event based on reason, experience, or observation.

**technique** – a method or style in which something is done.

## Web Sites

To learn more about cool art, visit ABDO Publishing Company on the World Wide Web at **www.abdopublishing.com**. Web sites about cool art are featured on our Book Links page. These links are routinely monitored and updated to provide the most current information available.

# INDEX